AF584315

the book that grown-ups get wrong

Rove McManus

A Scholastic Australia Book

To Gav, Juls and Luke for helping me get this grown-up thing right –R.M.

Scholastic Australia
An imprint of Scholastic Australia Pty Limited
PO Box 579 Gosford NSW 2250
ABN 11 000 614 577
www.scholastic.com.au

Part of the Scholastic Group
Sydney • Auckland • New York • Toronto • London • Mexico City
New Delhi • Hong Kong • Buenos Aires • Puerto Rico

Published by Scholastic Australia in 2023.

A catalogue record for this book is available from the National Library of Australia

ISBN: 978-1-76120-499-9

Typeset in Questa Sans and Abril Text.

Book design by Nicole Stofberg. Art coloured by Nicole Stofberg.

Printed in China by RR Donnelley.
Scholastic Australia's policy, in association with RR Donnelley, is to use papers that are renewable and made efficiently from wood grown from responsibly managed sources, so as to minimise its environmental footprint.

10 9 8 7 6 5 4 24 25 26 27 / 2

This is the book that grown-ups get wrong.

Which is awkward, I know.
Because there's one reading it to you right now,
isn't there?

Like I said, awkward.

And I know it's all going well so far, but trust me.
They always, always get it wrong eventually.
Watch . . .

a penguin wearing a party hat!

There they go again.

Getting it wrong.

You might be thinking that maybe they just have a problem with frogs. But trust me, it's because grown-ups always get this book wrong.

Like, *always*.

Let's try something different this time. You'll see what I mean.

This one is super easy.

What's this?

Yep, it's obviously a . . .

tap-dancing hippo!

What? Ugh. They've done it again, haven't they? I was right. This always happens.

Does that really look like a tap-dancing hippo?

YES! Absolutely! Of course it does!

Wait, no it doesn't. Wrong again, silly grown-up, with your mixed-up, random ideas!

It's not a tap-dancing hippo. It's . . .

a unicorn with a horn made entirely out of eyebrows!

That one wasn't just wrong, it was a little creepy.

Fine. Whatever.

I know you think this grown-up is doing it on purpose, but I'm telling you, no matter how hard they try, every single grown-up gets this book wrong.

This is why grown-ups should never even be allowed to read this book in the first place. They will always get it wrong no matter how hard they . . .

Jump up and down singing Happy Birthday to the custard tart queen.

OK, now this is getting ridiculous.

Let's try something else.

Get the grown-up to close their eyes and you can explain what's on the next page. If this grown-up is going to keep getting this book wrong, it's up to you to get it right for them. So without saying exactly what it is, describe what you see on the next page, and have them open their eyes when you are done.

Here we go . . .

Now, ask them what they think you described.

Pretty obvious, right?

It’s . . .

a skeleton doing the tango with a duck on its head!

You know what?

Maybe we should just accept that sometimes

grown-ups aren't as smart as you

and sometimes are just going to get things wrong.

Like this picture of . . .

the Five-eyed mayor of the Cheese Planet Glooboolooo.

But just because they get it wrong,
doesn't mean we can't still enjoy this book.
We'll just have to soldier on

no matter what they say.

How about we try and go faster?

Here we go . . .

This is a

fairy teaching a dragon mathematics.

Wow.

Denise
the juggling
dinosaur.

Look!
It's Pancake Pete who
has maple syrup for
hair and a pet dog
made out of waffles.

In fact . . .

Here's Captain Twinklepants, the curly-wurly, cutie-pie, left-handed space pony with a glittery purple spatula that she only uses every second Blurpsday of the broccoli moon, singing a heavy metal sea-shanty about the magnificent belly-dancing antics of Dave the ninja.

Right! That's it!

It's one thing to get a book wrong, but if you grown-ups are not going to take getting it wrong seriously, then let's just forget about this completely!

I'll just leave you here to look at this . . .

frog.

Wait a second. What was that they just said?
Did I just hear them correctly?
Did they just get that . . . *right*?

They did?

Let's try again, just to be sure.

Here’s an owl.

A panda.

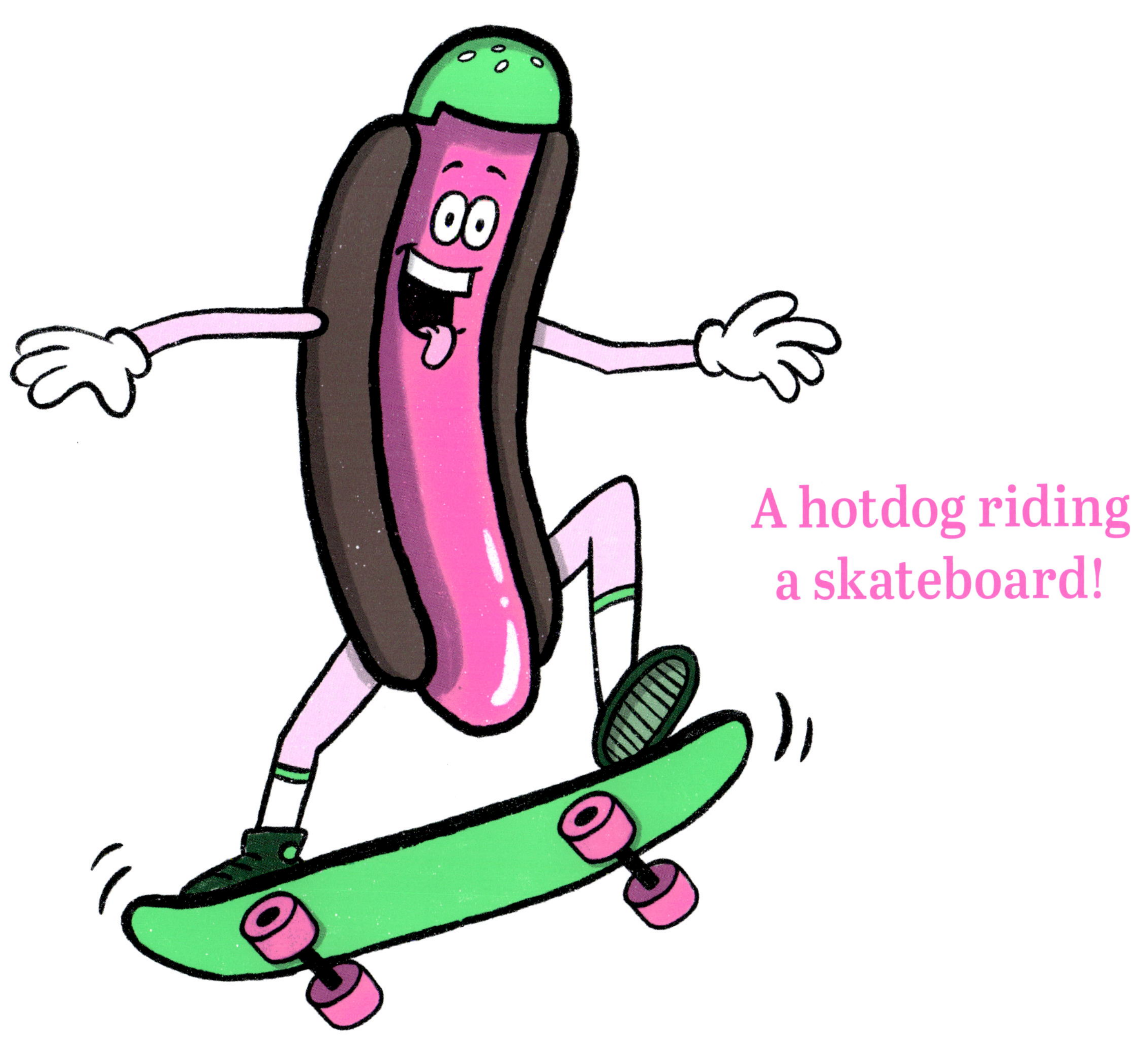

A hotdog riding
a skateboard!

(Ok, that last one was a trick one!)

But they got it right!

Now we can celebrate because grown-ups won't get this book wrong anymore!

Phew.

That wasn't so hard was it?

Thanks for all your help.
It looks like they've got it now.

So, like I was saying, I'll just leave you here to look at this . . .

frog.

This cute, little, green frog
that we all know says . . .

SHRIMP BISCUIT!

OH NO!

Looks like we have to go back to the start and train them all over again.